ANDREW MUÑOZ

SELECTED PAINTINGS

2007 - 2014

ISBN-13:978-1508424253
ISBN-10:150842425X

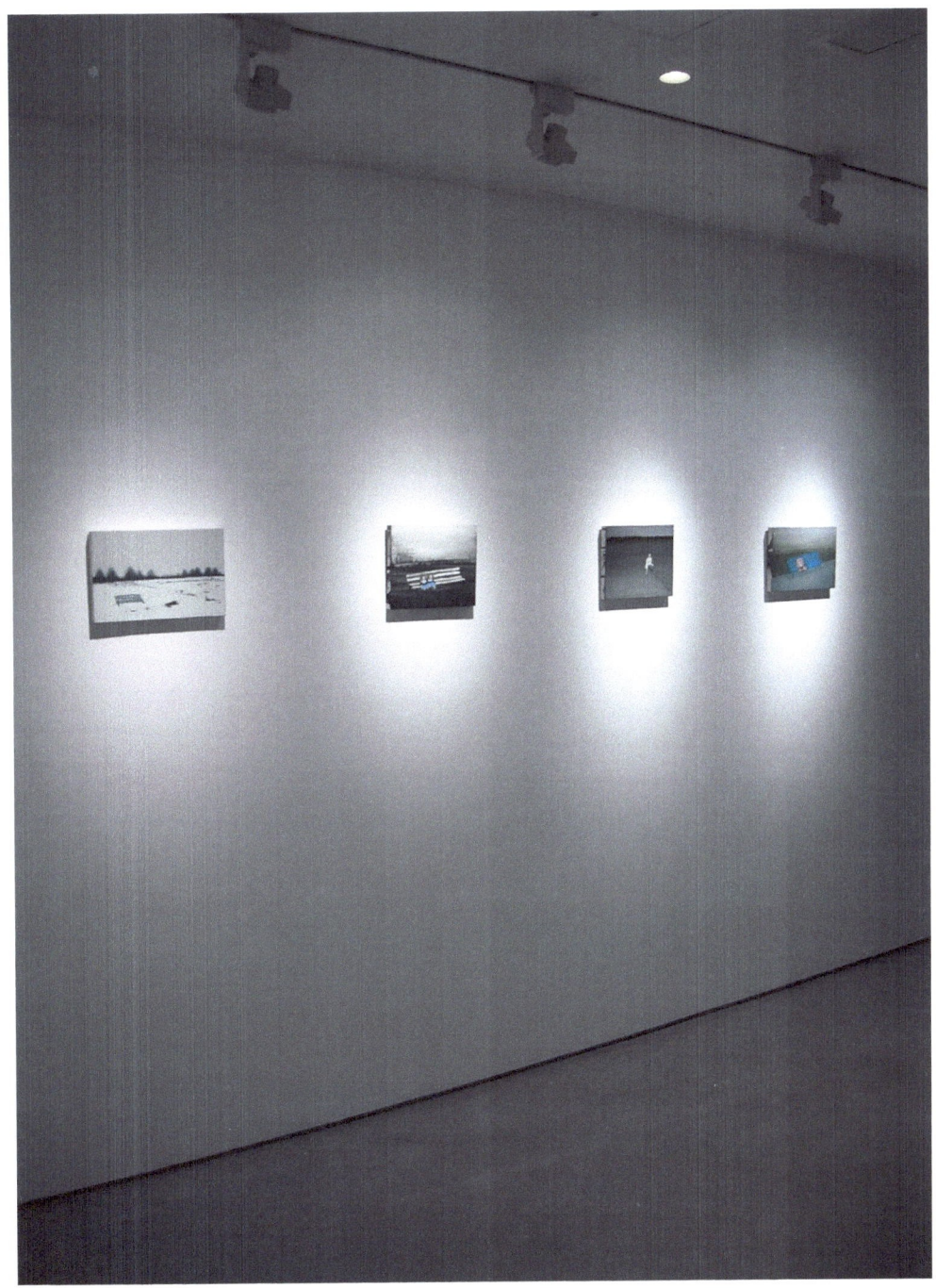

Preceding page: Installation of solo show at Andipa Contemporary, London, March 2012

These selected works are not intended to be read as allegories or parables, but rather as personal, instinctive responses to my own sensibilities surrounding the darker side of humanity. The narratives that often form the 'triggers' for the paintings have varied origins, a childhood memory, a response to an existing image or news item, my own photography or a witnessed event.

Allowing the material of the paint to evolve the work, these initial narratives are lost during the process of painting and others inevitably emerge in their place. The figures and the 'landscapes' also evolve and transform into something hopefully recognisable to the viewer, not only to the eye, but to the imagination.

These figures represent characters or psychological 'models' which I relate to on some level and which I feel allude to certain universal primitive conditions which are perhaps only thinly disguised by the social veneer. I imagine the figures are fictional characters wandering around trying to fit into their own versions of reality.

Andrew Muñoz 2015

Bluebirds
2007
Oil on canvas
35x60cms

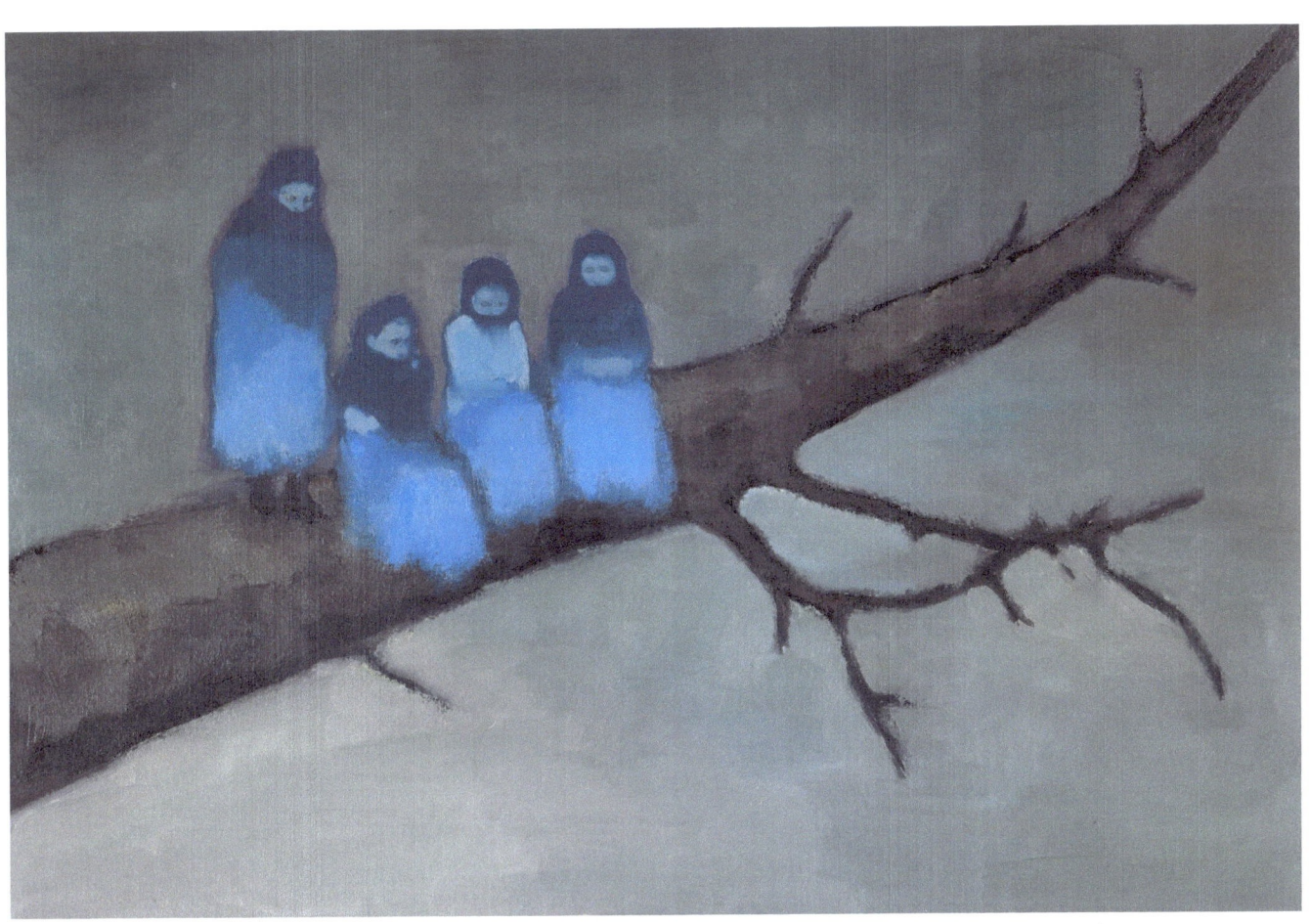

Hum
2007
Oil on board
70x60cms

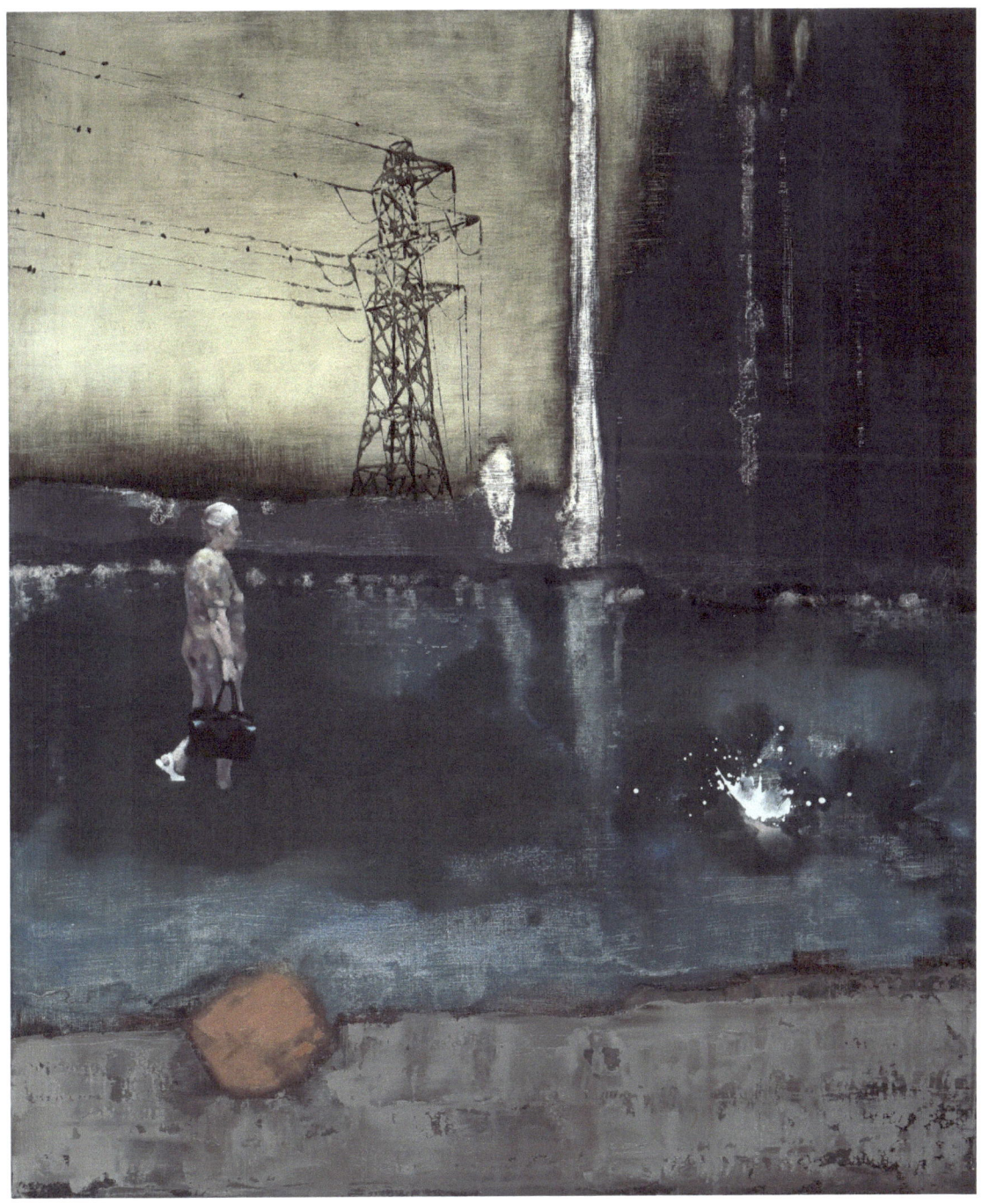

Grub 1 (Cautionary Tales)
2008
Oil on paper
30x40cms

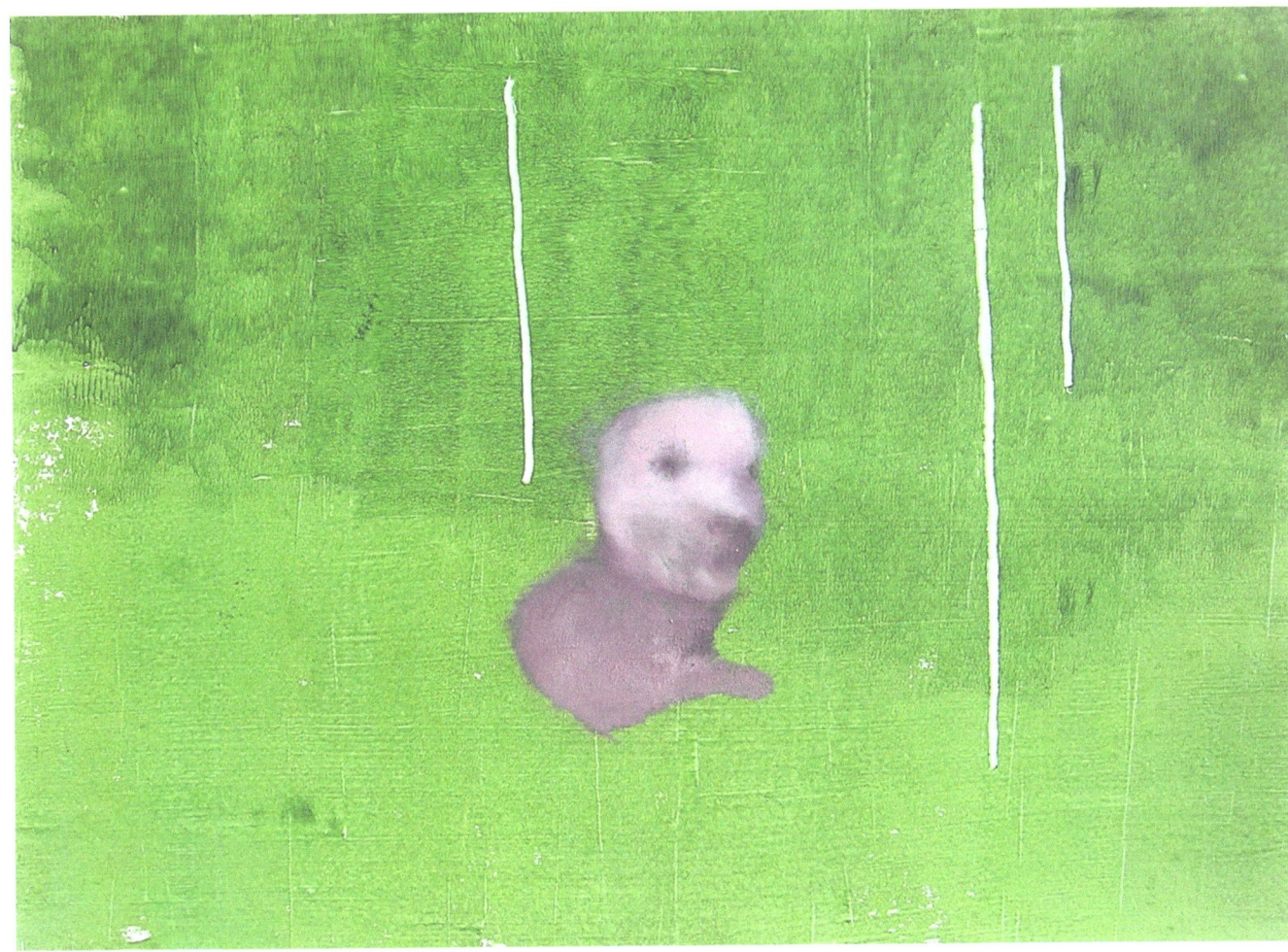

Upside-Down
2008
Oil on board
15x13cms

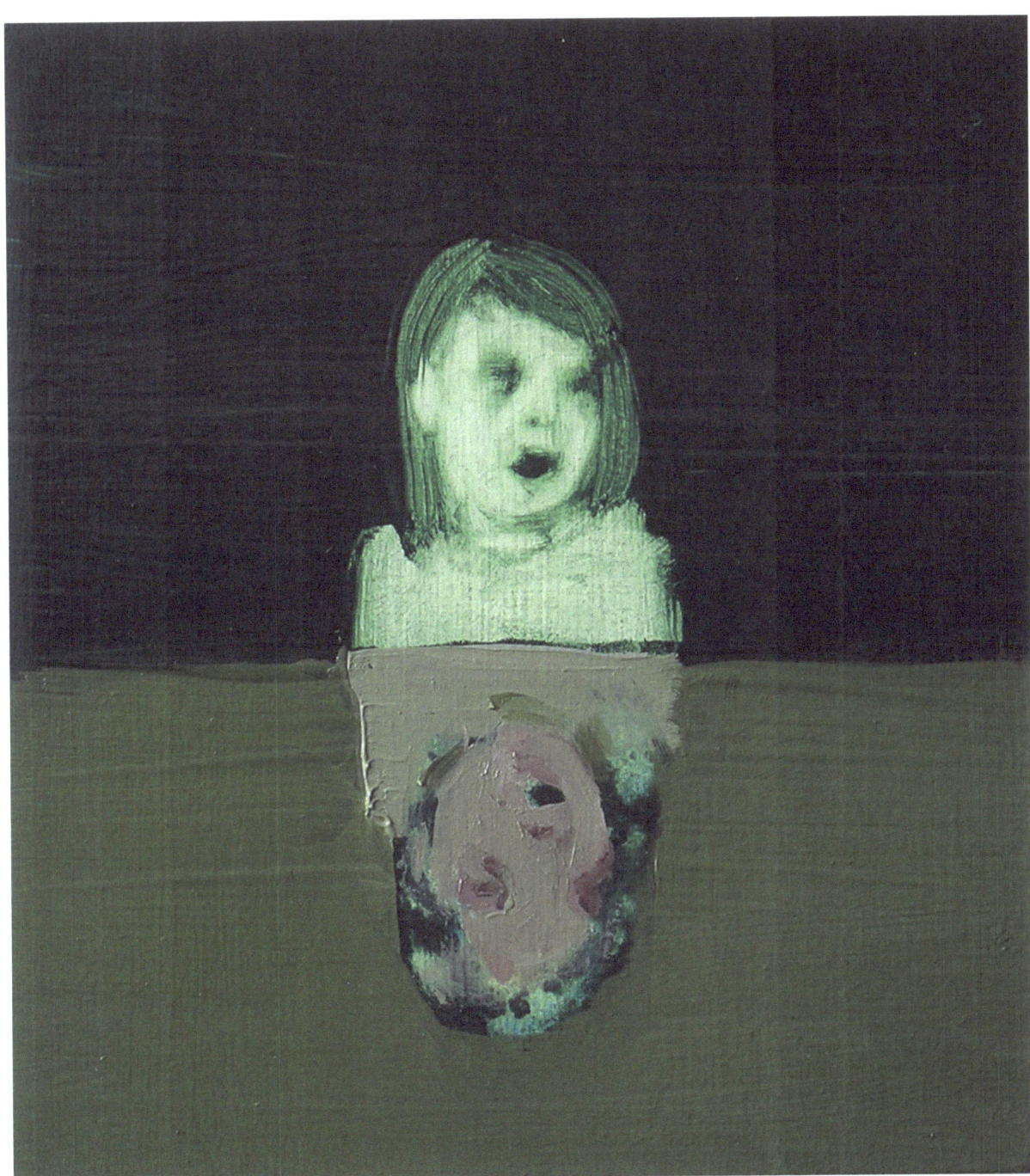

Towpath
2008
Oil on board
63x63cms

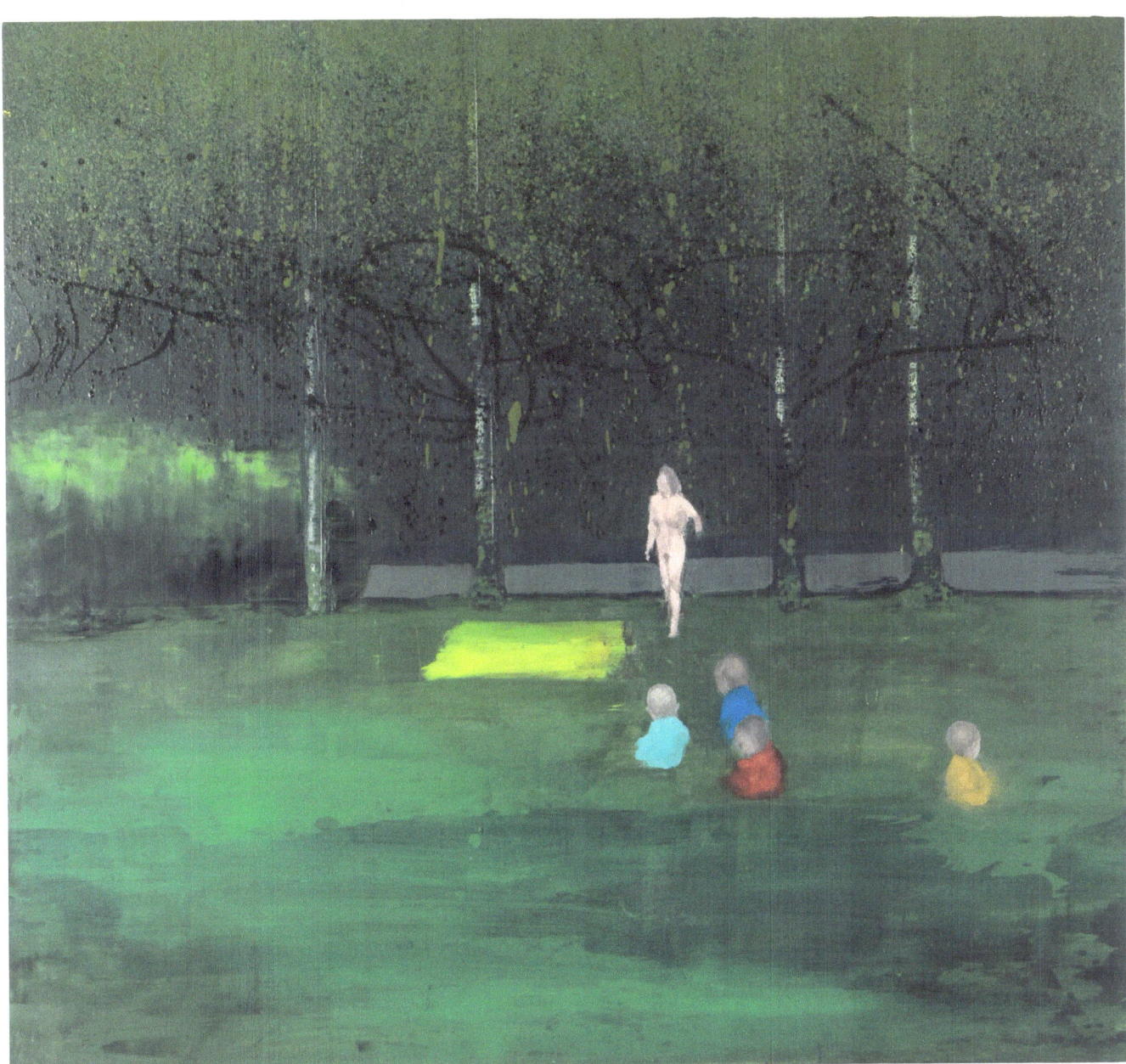

Pitch
2008
Oil on canvas
42x60cms

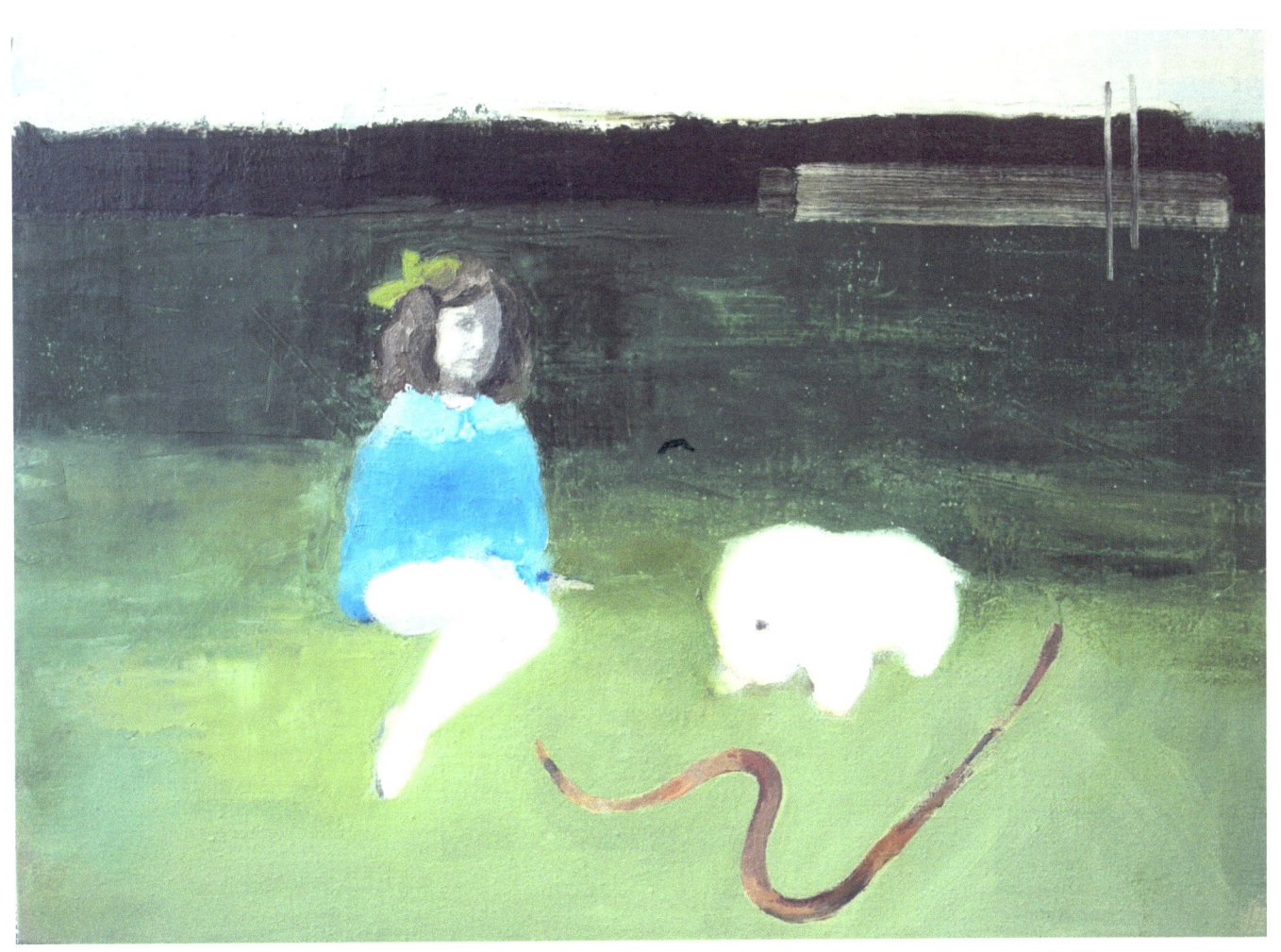

A Foolish Prank
2009
Oil on canvas
60x60cms

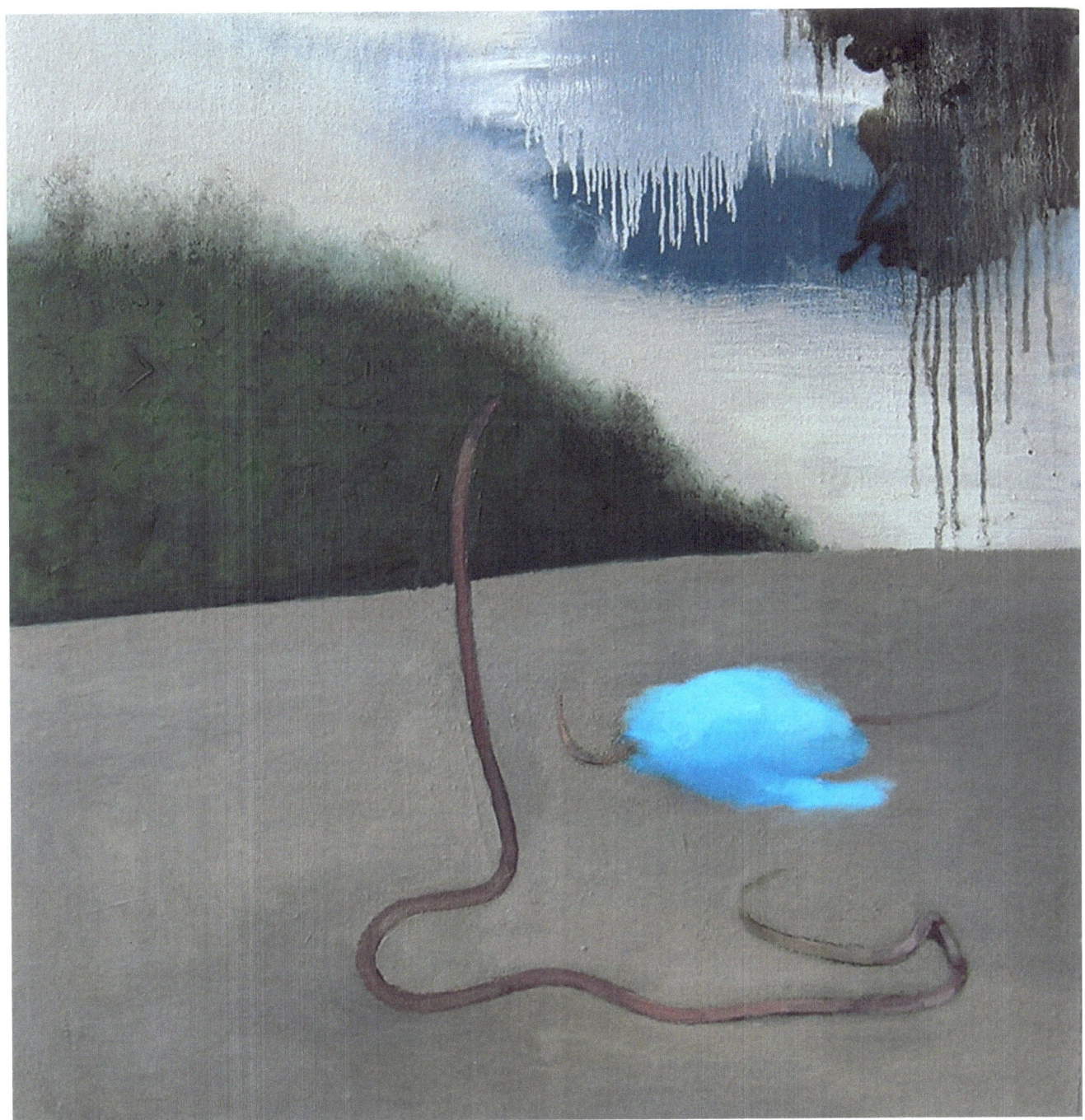

Sunrise (Monument)
2008
Oil on board
34x48cms

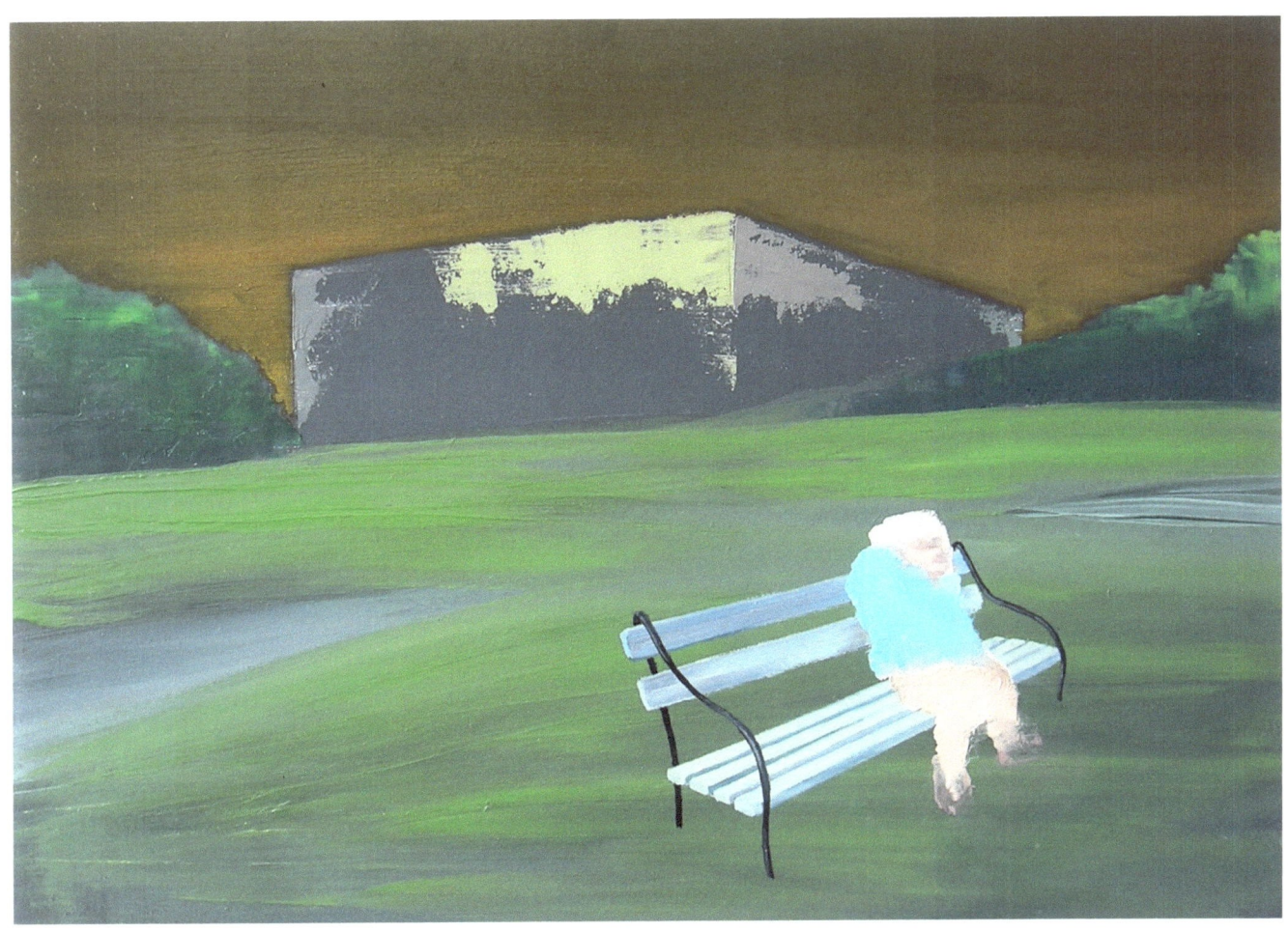

Memorial
2008
Oil on board
15x13cms

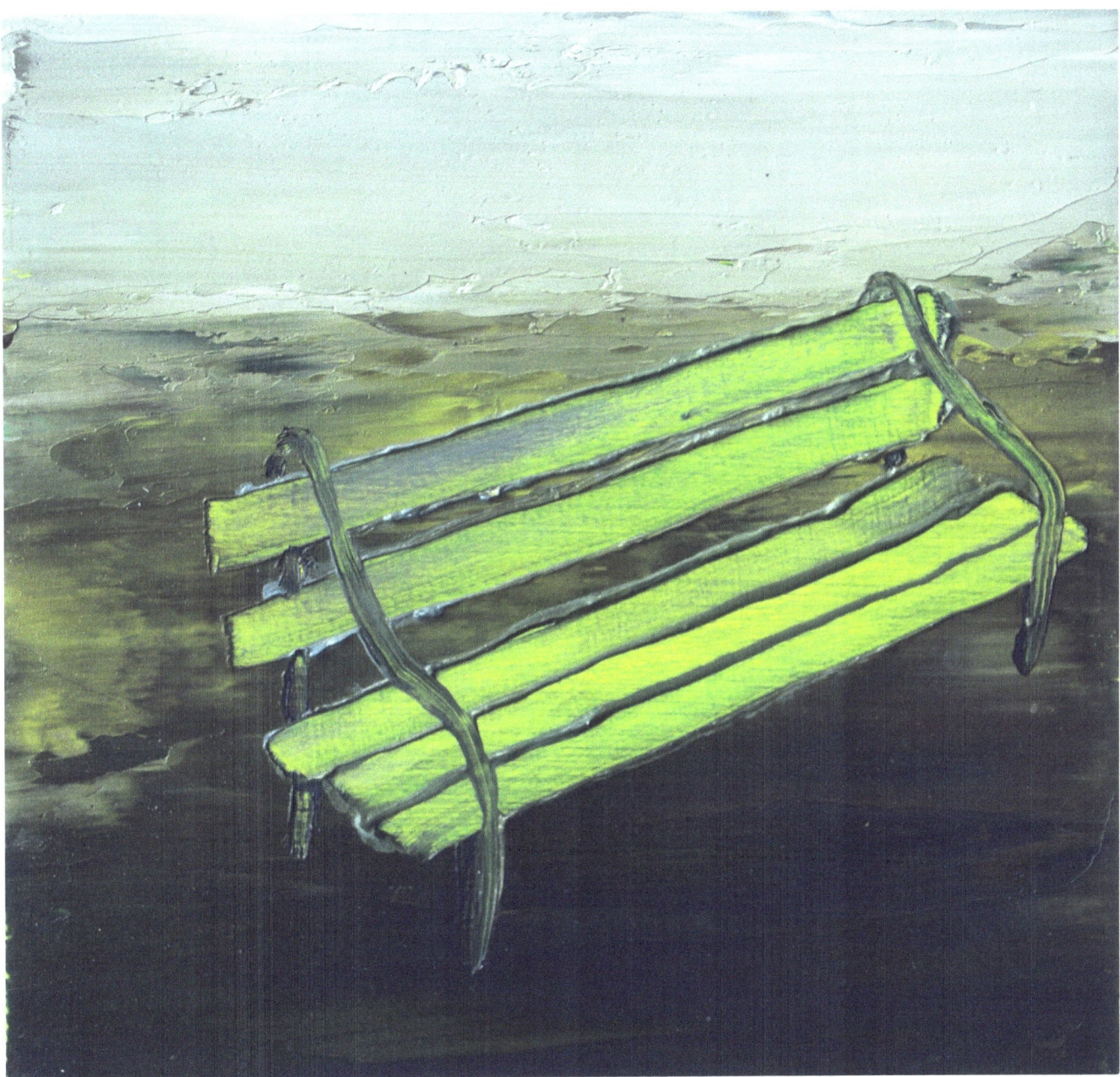

Las Gemelas
2008
Oil on board
22x36cms

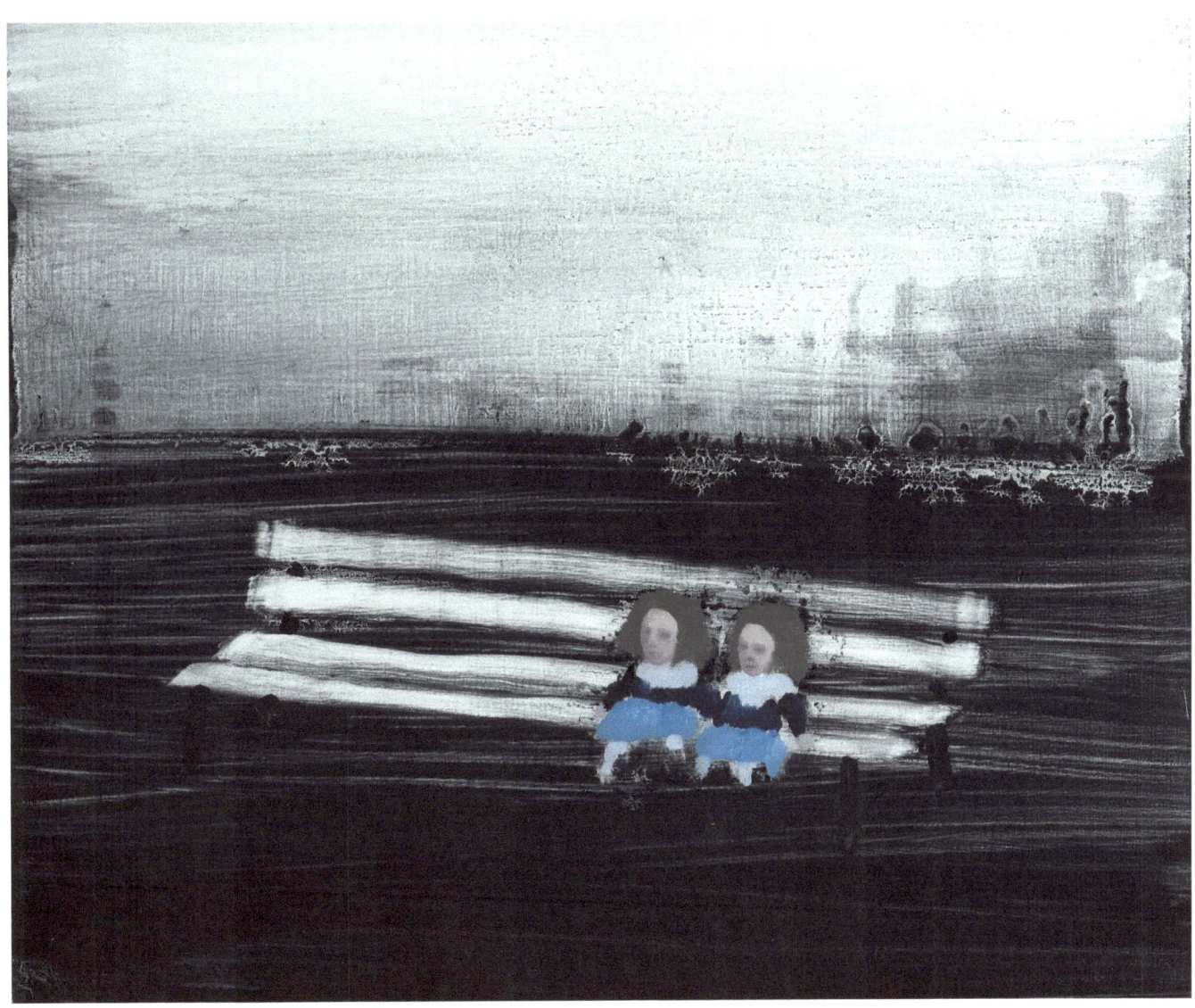

Dead Dog
2010
Oil on board
22x36cms

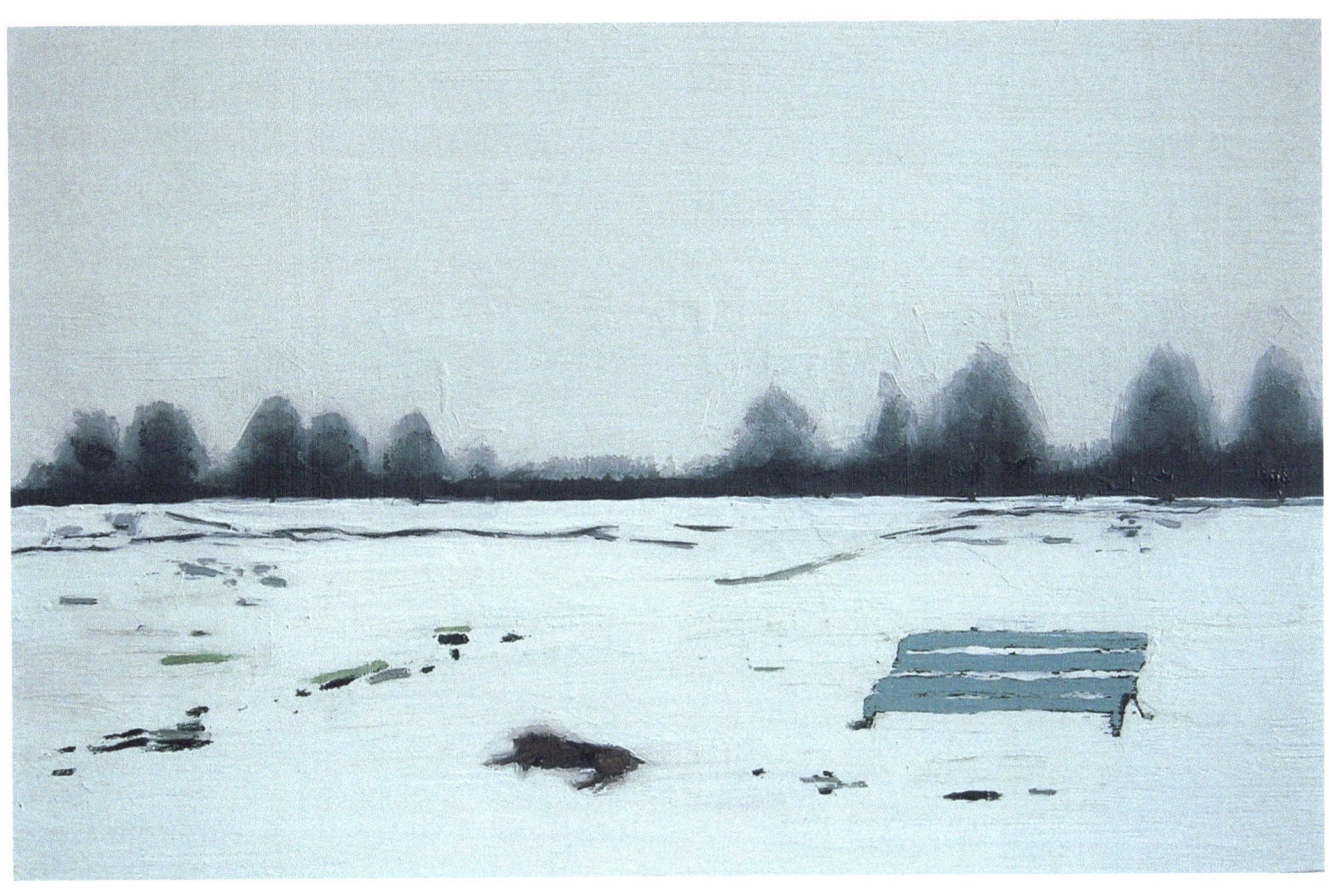

Monument
2008
Oil on board
44x44cms

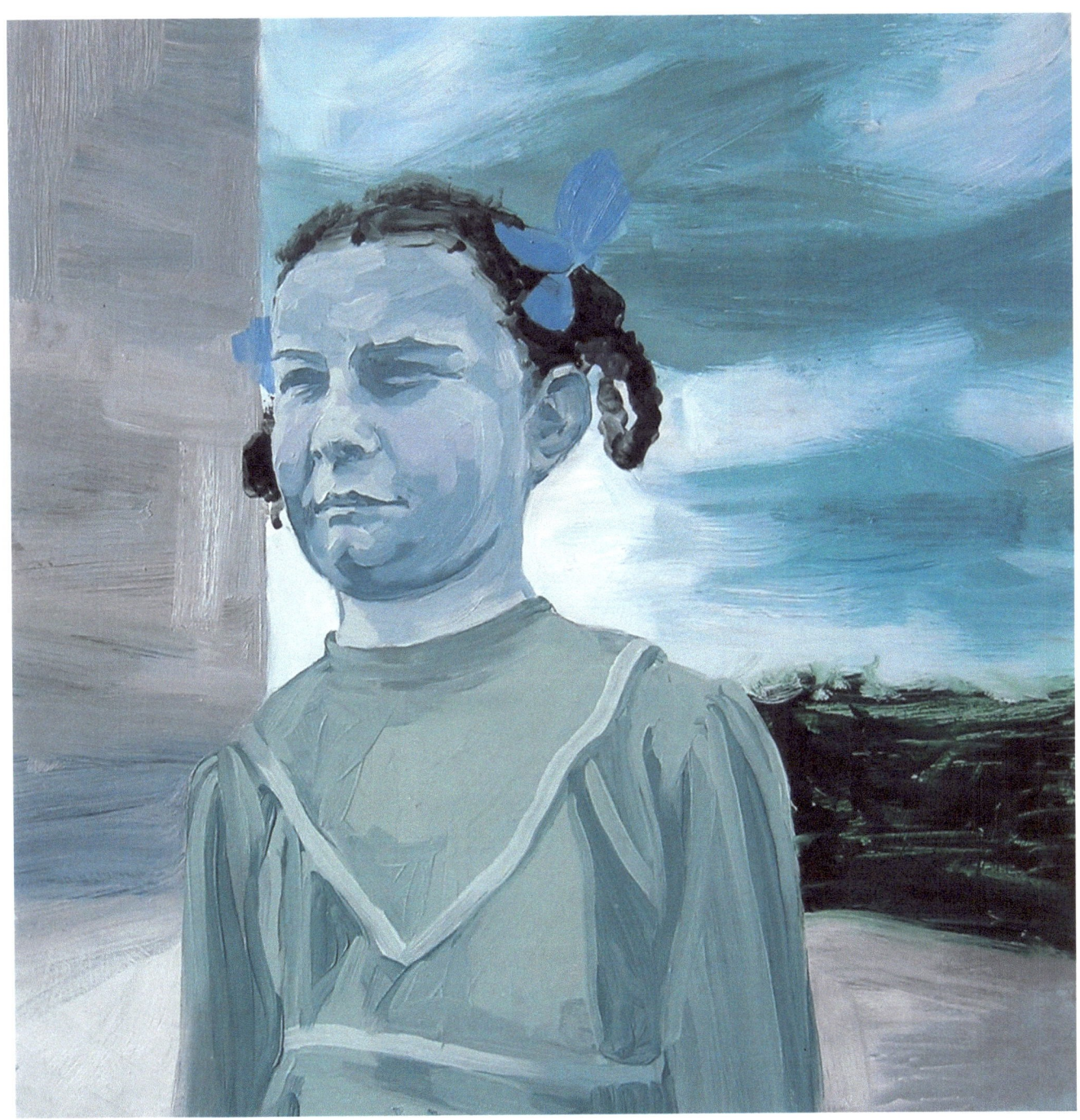

See-saw
2009
Oil on board
23x30cms

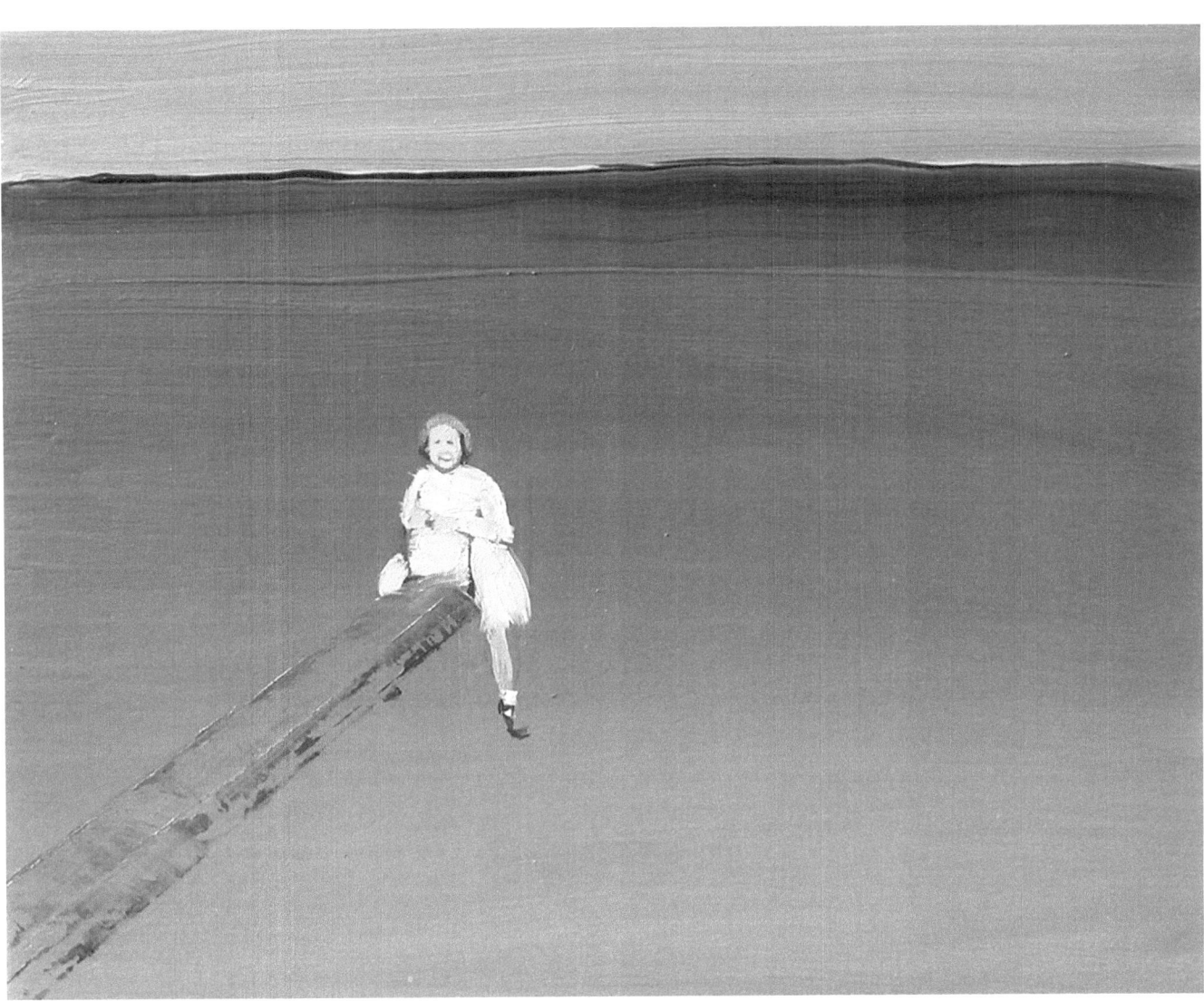

Das Kind
2010
Oil on canvas
160x110cms

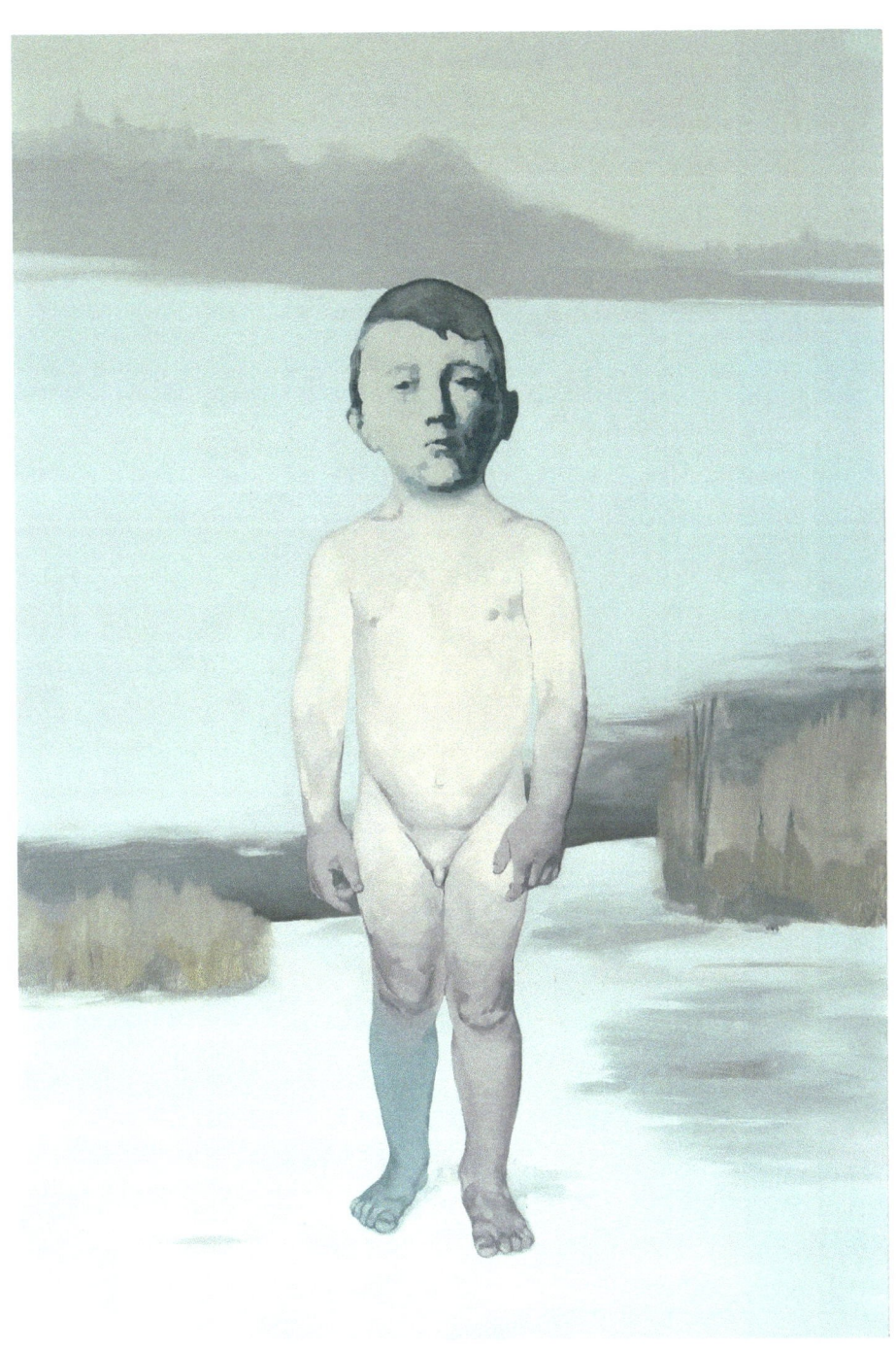

The Bather
2013
Oil on canvas
100x67cms

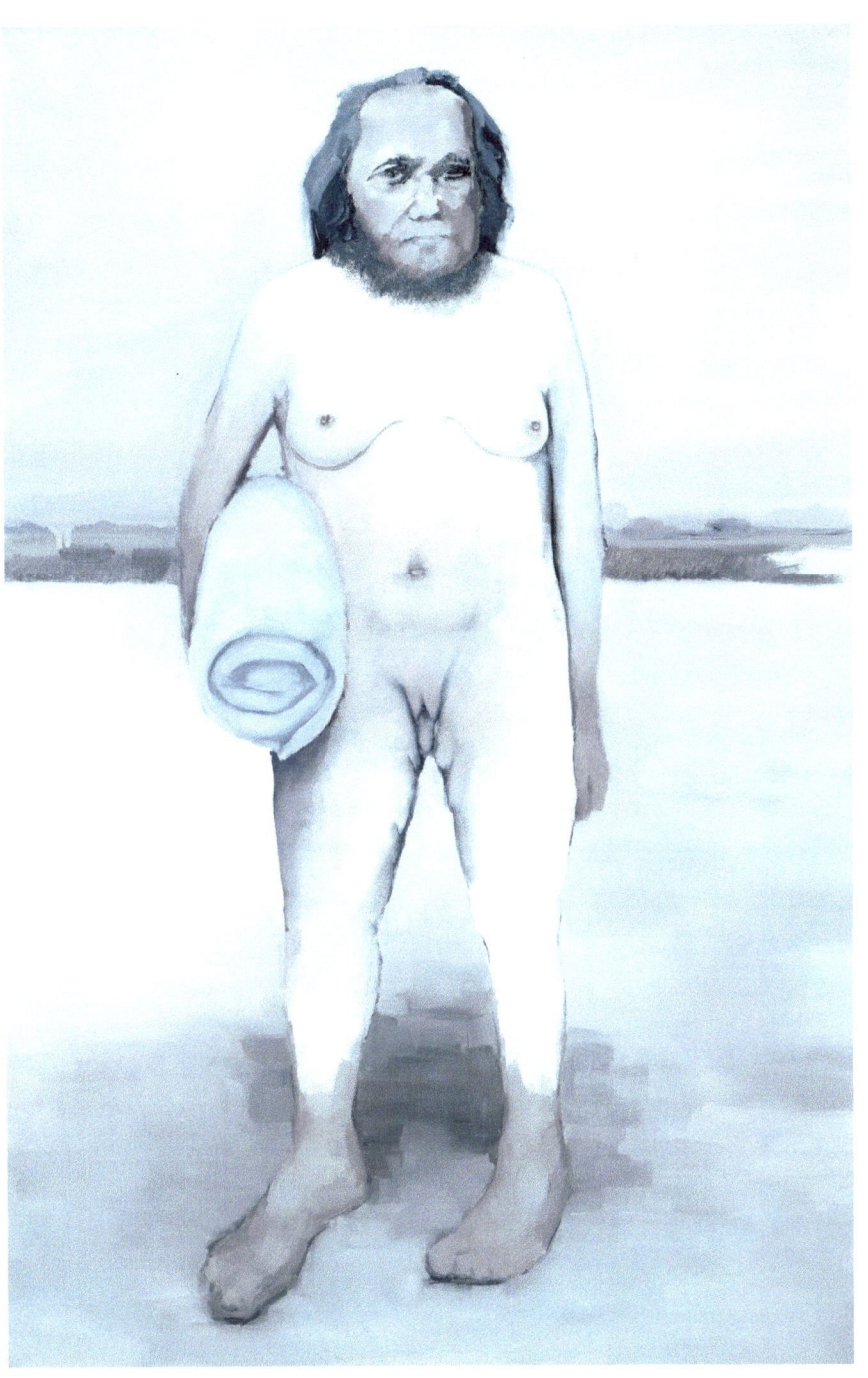

Wavey Davey
2013
Oil on board
16x16cms

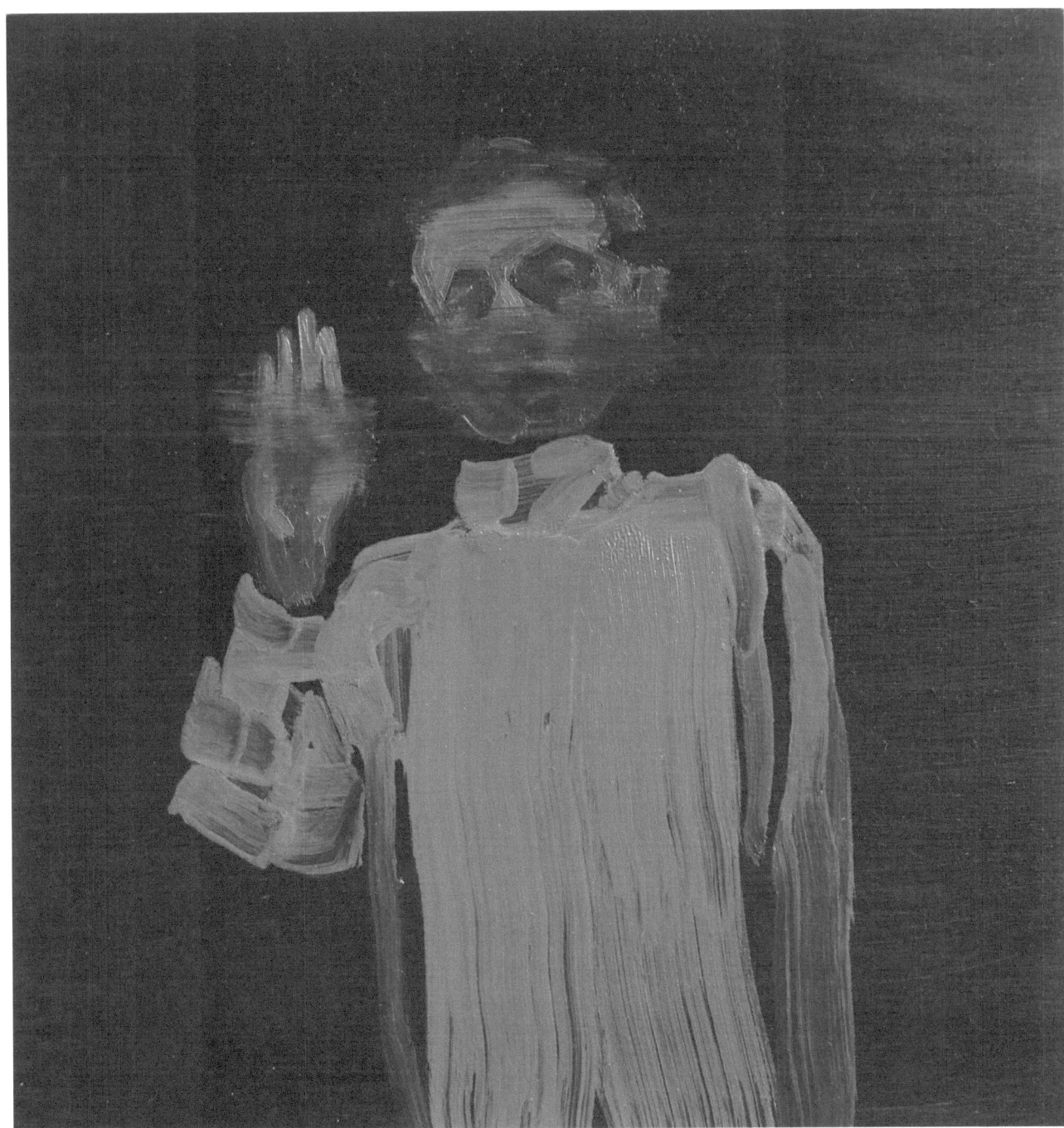

Seated Woman
2012
Oil on paper
29x20cms

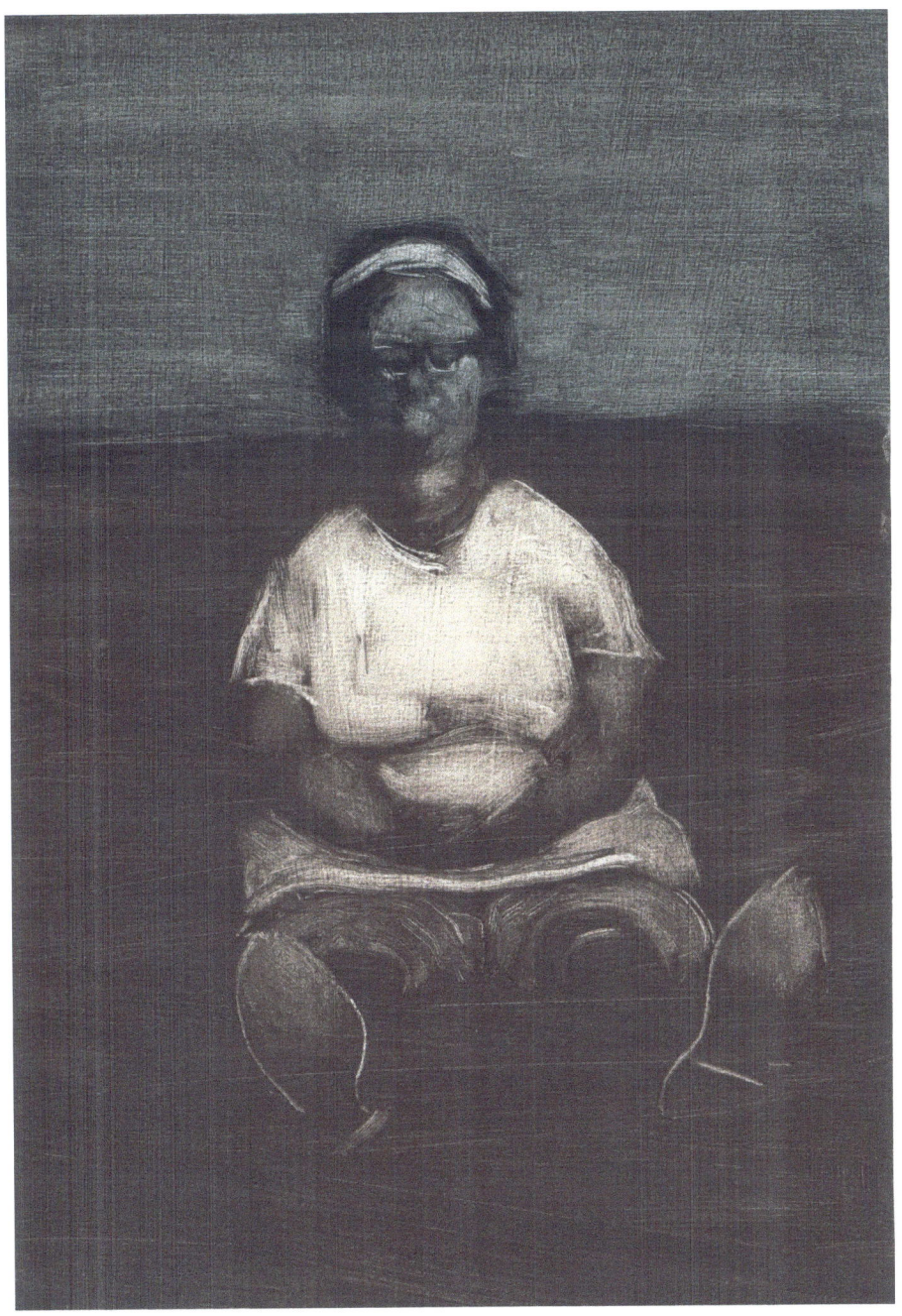

Hymnologist
2013
Oil on board
32x33cms

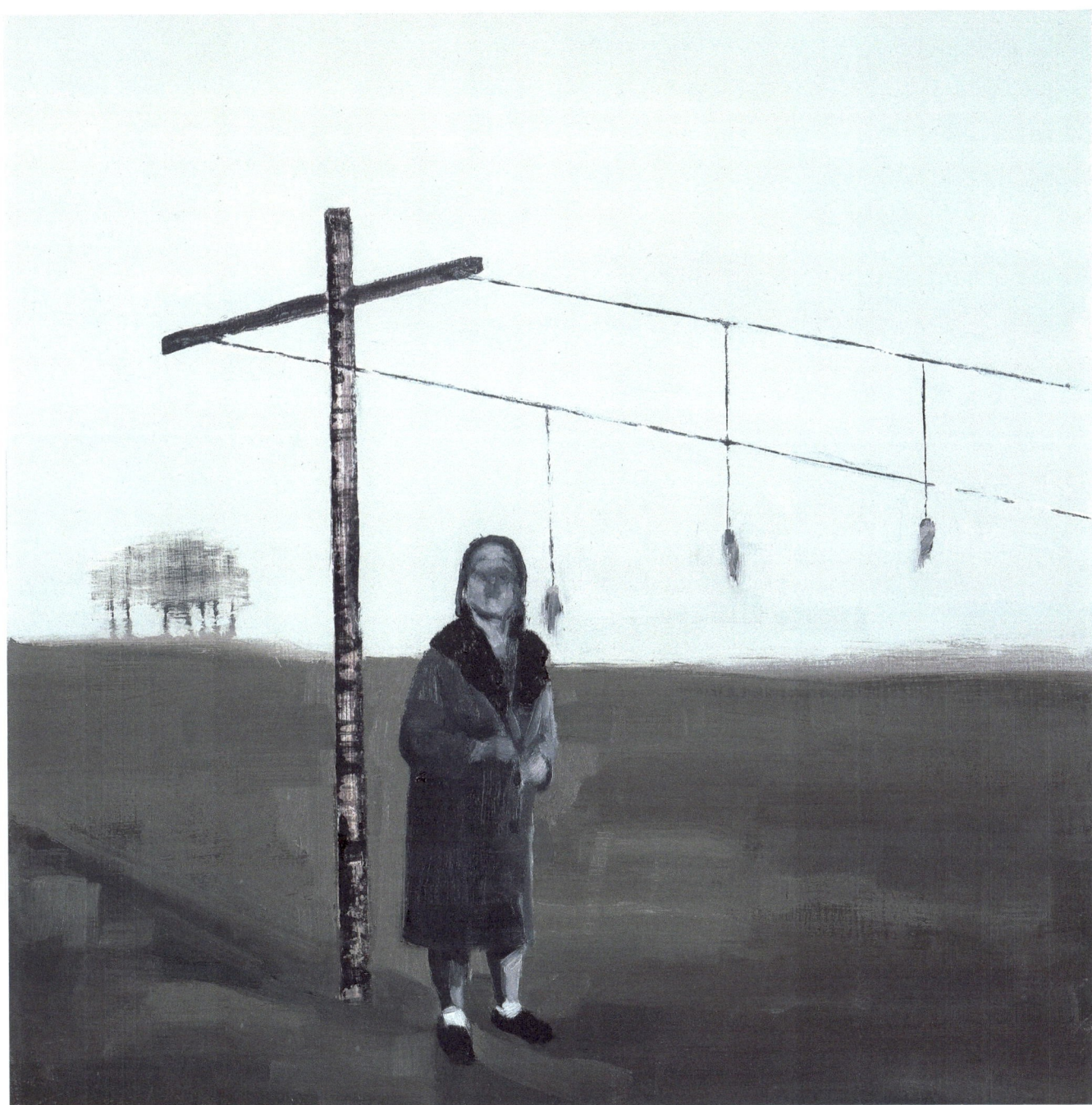

Ablution
2013
Oil on board
33x34cms

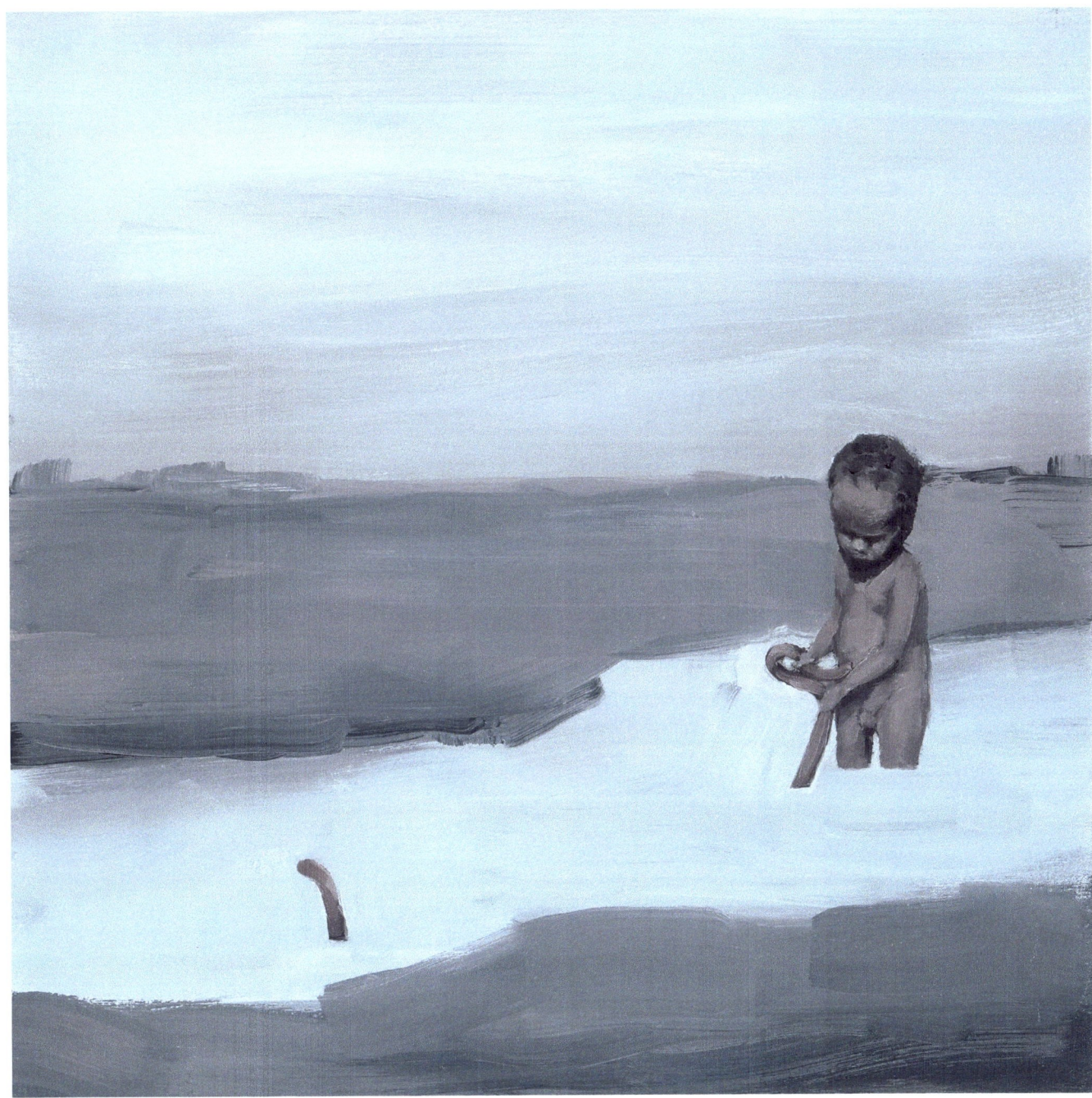

Boy with Dog
2013
Oil on board
16x16cms

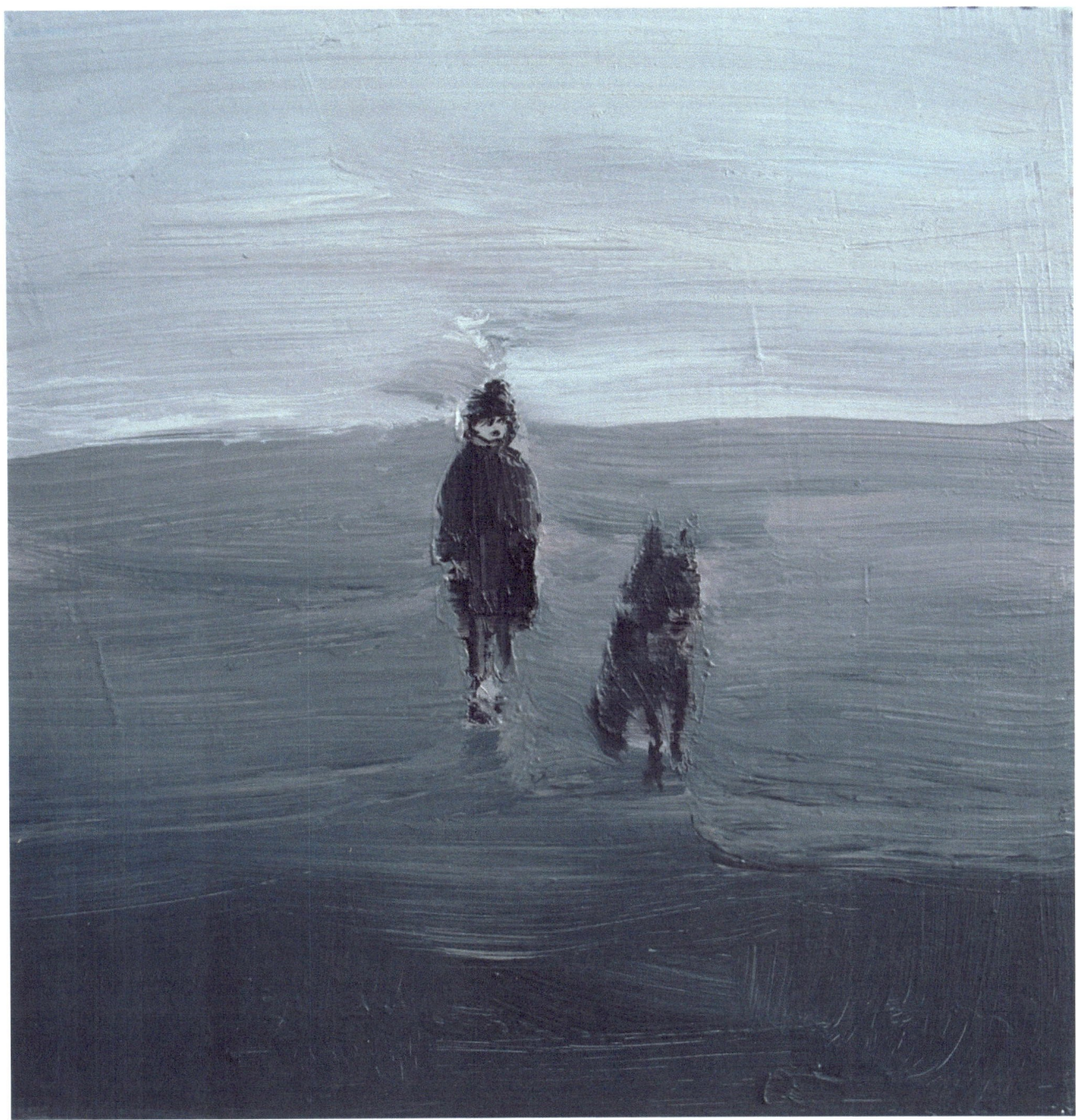

Auto-baptism
2014
Oil on canvas
101x101cms

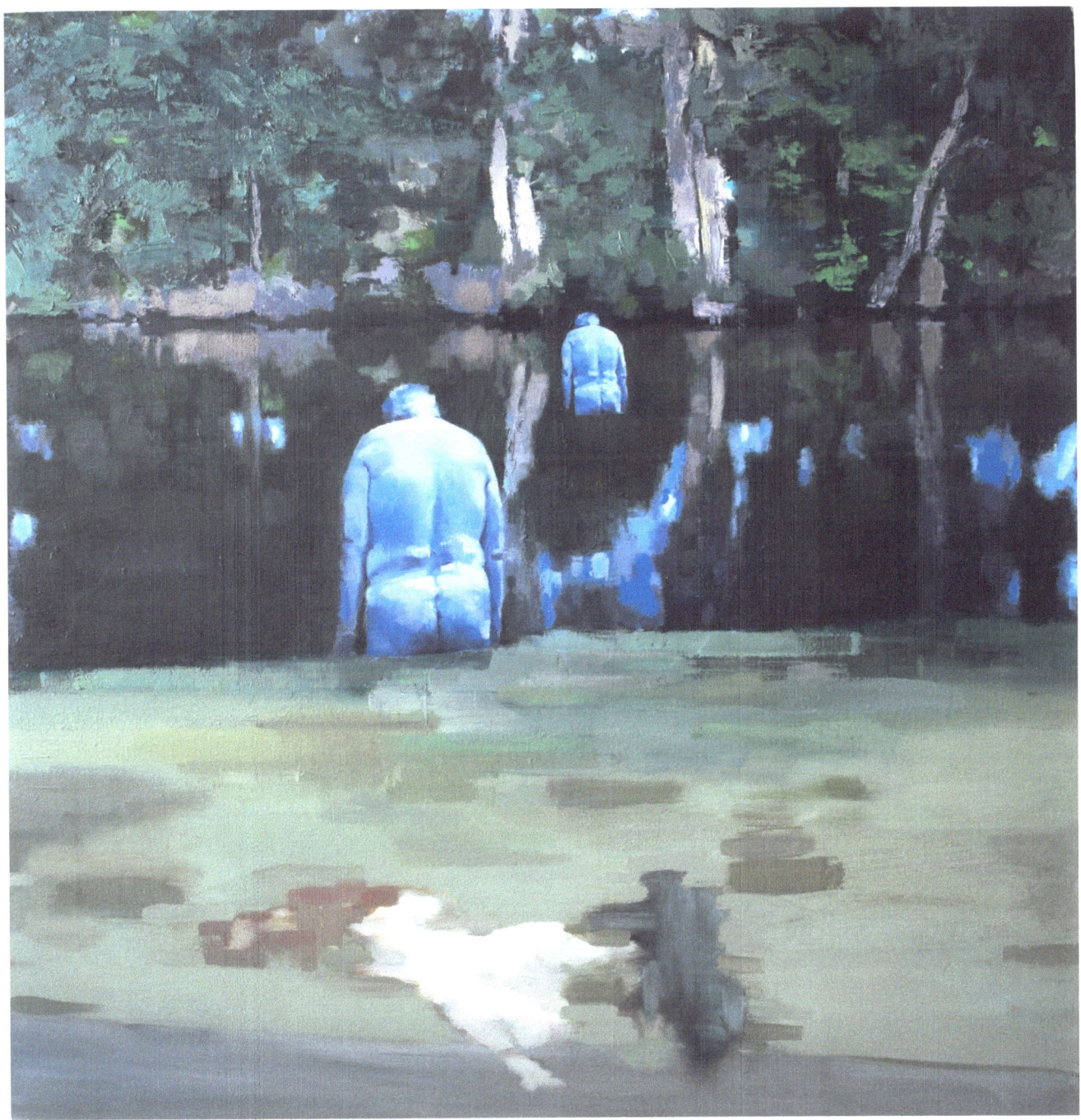

Where the Dead Live
2013
Oil on canvas
51x76cms

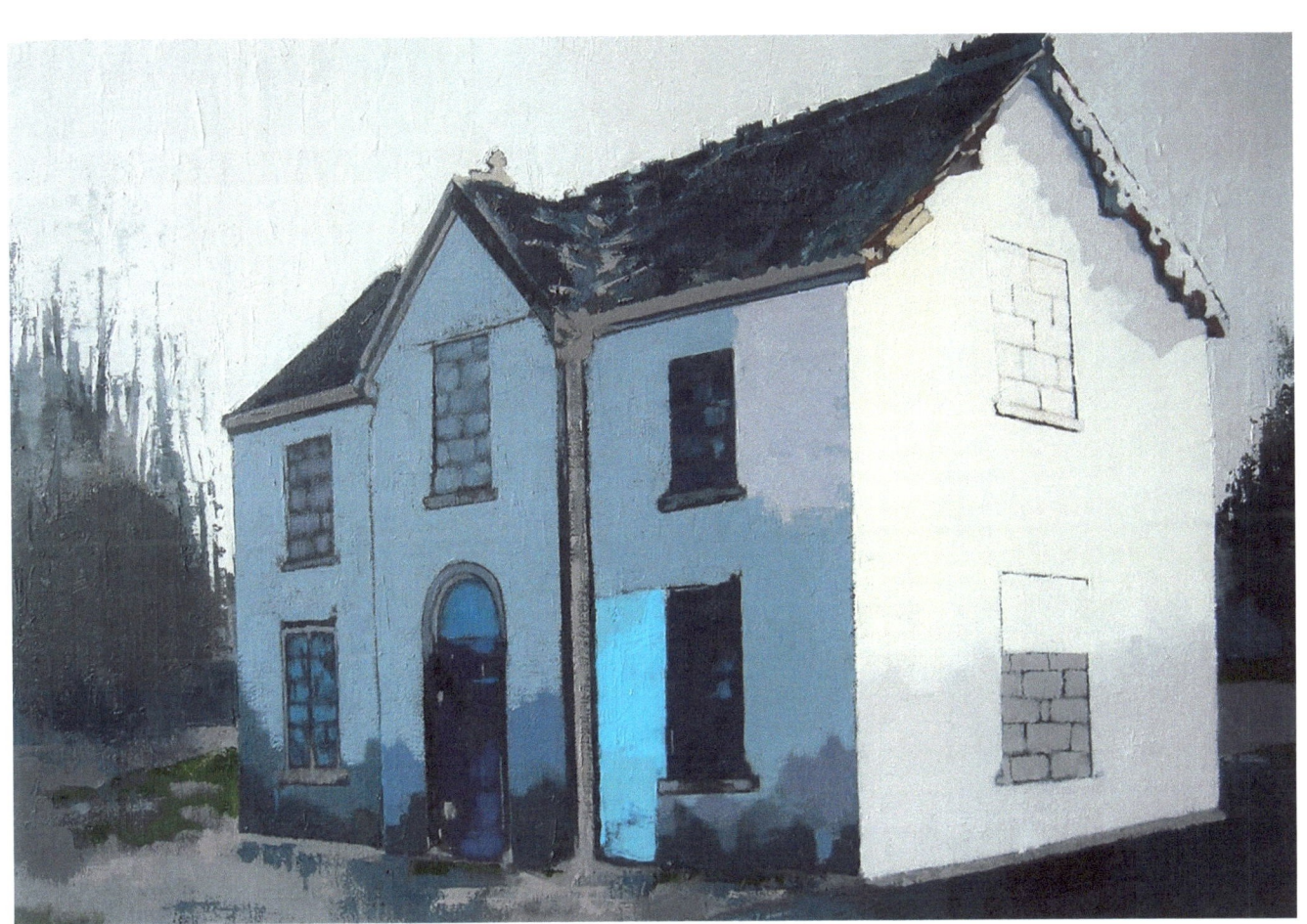

Opposite: Andrew Muñoz in his studio September 2013

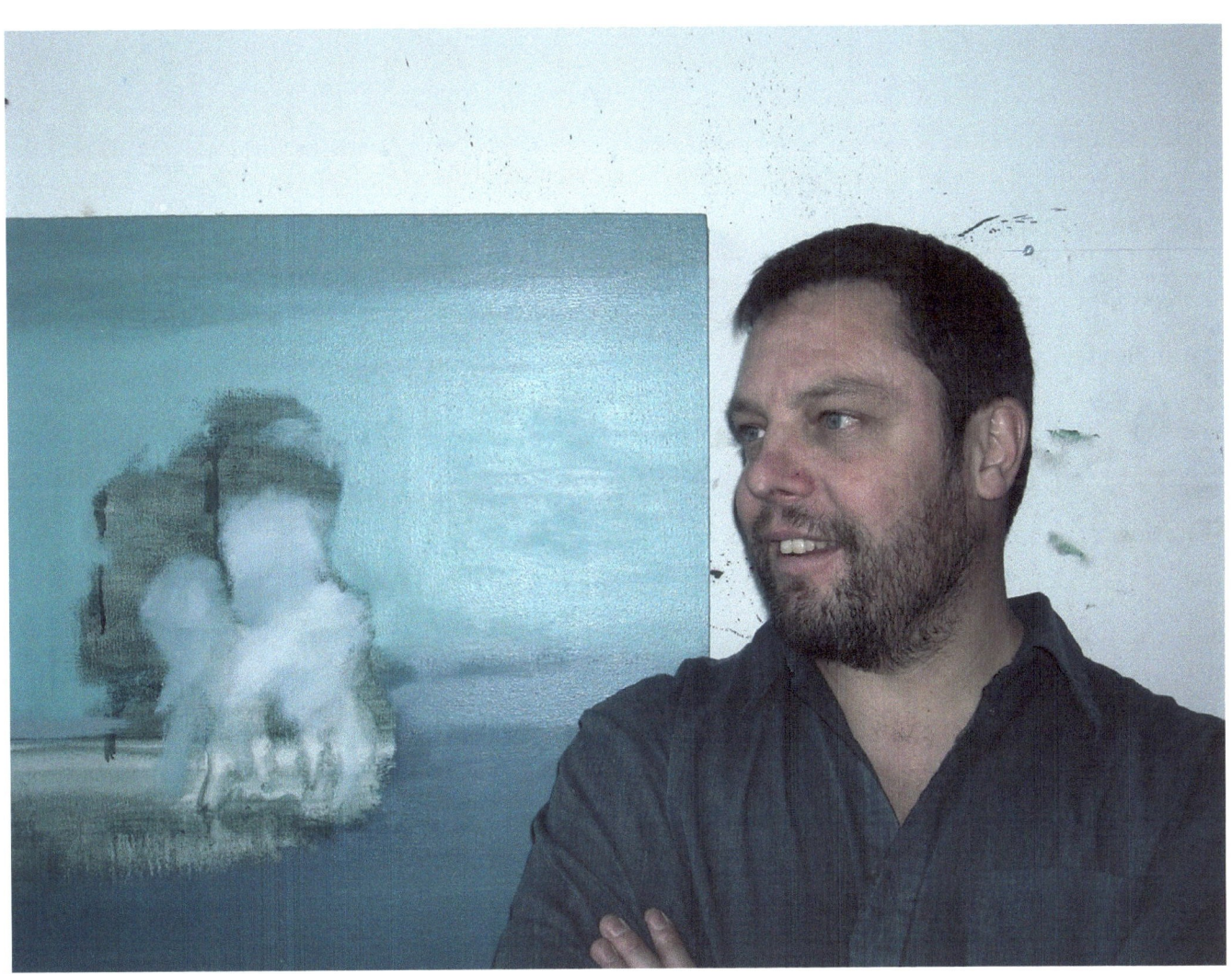

Biography:

Andrew Munoz was born in London in 1967 and studied at Plymouth College of Art (1995 – 1997), and Falmouth College of Art (1997 – 2000). He lives and works in Bristol, England.

Solo exhibitions:

2000 The Lane Gallery, Plymouth, UK – 2002 Flying Colours Gallery, London, UK – 2008 'Violare', Red Propeller Gallery, Devon, UK - 2012 A Walk in the Park, Andipa Contemporary, London, UK - 2015 British Contemporary Painters - Marylebone Crypt, London, UK - 2015 Recent Paintings, Royal West of England Academy, Bristol, UK

Selected group exhibitions:

2001 20/21 British Art Fair, Royal College of Art, London, UK – 2002 ART2002, London, UK – 2003 AAF, Commonwealth Centre, London, UK - 2004 South West Arts, Pheonix Art Centre, Exeter, UK - 2005 SWA, Royal Albert Museum, Exeter, UK – 2005 Atkinson Gallery, Liverpool, UK - 2006 'Encore' RWA, Bristol, UK – 2006 'Hide and Seek', Mivart Studios, Bristol, UK – 2007 'Homecoming', Southbank Arts - Bristol, UK 2008 'Lost and Found', Plymouth College of Art, Plymouth, UK 2008 'Bite', Centrespace, Bristol, UK 2008 'Vinespace', Vyner Street, London – 2008 Autumn Open, RWA, Bristol, UK - 2009 Red Propeller Gallery, Devon, UK - 2010 RWA, Bristol, UK - 2011 RWA, Bristol, UK - 2012 Andipa Contemporary, London, UK - 2012 'Drawn', RWA, Bristol, UK - 2013 British Contemporary Painters, Marylebone Parish Church Crypt, London, UK – 2013 Academician selection exhibition, RWA, Bristol, UK – 2014 'Scape', View Gallery, Bristol, UK – 2014 Contemporary British Painters, (Priseman-Seabrook Collection), Huddersfield Art Gallery, UK – 2014 @Paintbritain, Ipswich Art School Gallery, UK – 2015 'Drawn', RWA, Bristol, UK

Publications:

2008 PROOF Magazine (April)
2014 Evolver Magazine (January/February)
2014 Contemporary British Painters (Priseman-Seabrook Collection at Huddersfield Art Gallery)
2014 @PaintBritain, Ipswich Art Gallery
2015 Evolver Magazine (Main feature May/June)

Prizes/Awards:

The Edwards Painting Prize 2007
Bristol Fine Art Award 2008
Royal West of England Academician 2014

Public Collections:

Lakeland Art Trust, Abbots Hall, Cumbria, UK
Swindon Art Gallery and Museum, UK
Royal West of England Academy, Bristol, UK
Madison Museum of Fine Art, Atlanta, USA

www.ingramcontent.com/pod-product-compliance
Lightning Source LLC
Chambersburg PA
CBHW050900180526

45159CB00007B/2741